DISCIPLINE FOR MORAL GROWTH

by Marilyn Watson

CSEE
2007

DISCIPLINE FOR MORAL GROWTH
by Marilyn Watson

We gratefully acknowledge Jossey-Bass/a Wiley Imprint for permission to reprint passages from *Learning to Trust: Transforming Difficult Elementary Classrooms Through Developmental Discipline*, by Marilyn Watson and Laura Ecken (2003).

The selection from "Taking a Believing Stance" (2002) is reprinted by permission of Joy L. Pelton, Lecturer, Department of Teacher Education, California University at Sacramento.

Special thanks to Laura Ecken and her former students for giving of their time and being willing to share their opinions, experiences, and knowledge.

Copies of this and other CSEE publications are available through

The Council for Spiritual and Ethical Education
PO Box 19807
Portland, Oregon 97280

See purchase information at www.csee.org

ISBN: 0-9778934-4-8

Contents

Preface 5

Introduction 7

First Principle: Build Warm, Caring, Trusting
Teacher-Student Relationships 9

Barriers to Building Warm, Caring,
Trusting Teacher-Student Relationships 10
Structural Barriers 10
Teachers' Beliefs About Why Children Misbehave 11
Students' Emotional Skills and Beliefs About
Themselves and Others 13

Overcoming Barriers to Warm, Caring,
Trusting Relationships 14
Structural Barriers 14
Teachers' Beliefs 15
Students' Beliefs 19

Second Principle: Support/Encourage Friendly
Relationships Among Students 24

Third Principle: Use Student Misbehaviors as
Opportunities for Social, Moral Instruction 27

The Problem with Punishment 30

Alternatives to Punishment 31
Academic Misbehavior: Failure to Do
Home or Classroom Assignments 33
Trust Violation: Stealing 37
Mistreatment of Peers: Name Calling or
Physically Harming Peers 41

Summary 46
References 49
About the Author 51

Preface

I lent my first copy of Marilyn Watson and Laura Ecken's *Learning to Trust* to my daughter, a first-grade teacher in a school not greatly unlike Laura Ecken's. Another project needed attention, and I planned to return to my reading upon its completion. I did not foresee the weeks of wait required for the book's return: not a comment on Marie-Claire's reading speed, but rather testimony to the power of *Learning to Trust*'s message regarding classroom management techniques that bond children to a classroom and school community while nurturing their autonomy and competence.

Dr. Watson's time spent with CSEE's Moral Development Team has offered us deeper insights into how much sense Developmental Discipline makes in schools whose missions entail social, emotional, and moral growth.

We asked Marilyn Watson to write this booklet for us because how we "do" discipline in our schools has such power to enhance—or undermine—our work to nurture ethical leadership for tomorrow's world. All educators are called upon to address children's misbehavior, but some approaches to discipline risk leaving children angry, frustrated, unwilling and uninterested in caring for others around them. We cannot risk the perilous side effects of such approaches. We are delighted that Dr. Watson consented to our request.

As becomes clear in the text that follows, a fuller understanding of Developmental Discipline's ways and powers awaits the reader of Watson and Ecken's *Learning to Trust*. We recommend the book's compelling story as further reading, especially for elementary school teachers. However, Watson and Ecken have much to say to teachers of older students, also.

Discipline for Moral Growth is the second in CSEE's series of booklets designed to help our schools become "models of the possible" in education. Marilyn Watson once referred to her work with, and for, educators in the humble statement "I want to change the world." We join her wholeheartedly. Our schools are essential for the creation of a world that is sensitive, peaceful, and stubbornly ethical. We believe that Marilyn Watson's wisdom and empirically validated experience can help us take steps toward that end.

David Streight
Exective Director
Council for Spiritual and Ethcial Education

Introduction

Several years ago, I chronicled an elementary teacher's efforts at fostering the ethical as well as intellectual development of her students. Together, the teacher, Laura Ecken, and I described what she did to support her students' ethical development and how the students responded to her efforts (Watson & Ecken, 2003). Gradually, a caring community emerged in the classroom and the students appeared to grow ethically as well as intellectually. Years later, I had the pleasure of interviewing several of these students as high school freshmen and sophomores. While all of these students were classified as "at risk" in elementary school, most were not only academically successful in high school, they also had developed strong ethical selves. When asked how they would want to be described, nearly all referred to core ethical dispositions— kind, friendly, happy, respectful, honest, and hard working.

> *(I'm) sweet, caring. (I have) a head on (my) shoulders.*

> *I respect people. … I'm respectful to adults and to other people…… Not a trouble maker……I usually get along with people.*

> *(I'm) good, cool to be around, funny, nice, caring, respectful, honest.*

> *I'm somebody you can come talk to if you've got a problem. I won't go back and tell people.*

> *A hard worker. Wanting…Wanting to do more in the classroom. I like…I just want… the ability to do above what I think I can do.*

Interestingly, these students not only described themselves as ethical people, they also attributed much of their ethical development to their elementary school teacher.

I definitely learned how to read (in her class). And I love reading now. I learned to have self control. …I learned how to succeed. Like she would tell us to just go on even though you don't think you can make it, just keep going. I've learned a lot from her. But I think the biggest would be reading and how to control myself.

…she taught me not to judge people. Like if you see somebody and they're different from you… Don't judge them because there are people saying that they're weird. Just walk up to them, start talking to them, maybe they're just like you. That's why I don't judge people and that's cause of her. I believe that's a good thing.

Most elementary teachers hope to foster students' ethical development as well as their academic growth. However, they often lack familiarity with well established principles to guide their efforts. The reflections of these students coupled with existing research on children's social, emotional, and ethical development provide three guiding principles:

• Build warm, caring, trusting teacher-student relationships,

• Support and encourage friendly relationships among students,

• Use student misbehaviors as opportunities for social, moral instruction.

These three principles form the core of a unique approach to classroom discipline and management that has come to be called Developmental Discipline. It is *developmental*, because it is guided by what we know about children's developmental levels and tasks, and because it holds a view of children as biologically predisposed to learn and to become contributing members of their community.

Let us return to the students from Laura Ecken's class and look at each of the guiding principles of Developmental Discipline, first through their eyes and then through the lens of research.

First Principle
Build Warm, Caring, Trusting Teacher-Student Relationships

It may seem that arguing for warm, caring, trusting teacher-child relationships is like arguing for tasty, nutritious, affordable school lunches. Who would argue with either? However, it is difficult to feel warm and caring, let alone trusting, when children do not behave as we wish. It is even more difficult if we view children as primarily motivated by self-interest, the view that permeates most traditional approaches to discipline. One would feel the obligation to treat children humanely, just as one feels the obligation to treat prisoners humanely. One might feel warm and caring toward some children—those who have "earned our trust" through their good behavior—but not toward children in general and especially not toward children who regularly misbehave. The importance and rarity of teachers showing genuine interest in and care for students was mentioned over and over by the high school students.

> *(M)ost teachers now days…they don't make relationships with their students. (I)t's one year to be here and you're off.*

This student contrasts the relative lack of caring relationships in her high school life with her experience with her elementary school teacher.

> *She seemed like she cared. She just acted like… she wanted to know about your life and she seemed like she cared about you.*

The students realized that high school teachers had less time to form relationships, but still they believed that their teachers could have been more caring and that the failure to build relationships hindered their learning and enjoyment of school. Because elementary teachers have more time with their students, it is easier to get to know and care about each student individually and the class as a whole. Easier, however, does not mean easy.

Barriers to Building Warm, Caring, Trusting Teacher-Student Relationships

Structural Barriers

Some barriers to caring, trusting teacher-student relationships are structural. Large class sizes, departmentalized instruction, raised academic expectations, and high stakes testing can lead the conscientious and caring teacher to cut personal conversations short in favor of pushing on with the academic curriculum. There seems to be so little time, and so much content to cover. But taking the time for personal conversations and a willingness to help students with their personal as well as their academic problems were mentioned over and over by the students as central to feeling that their teacher really cared about them. Below are two examples of explanations offered by high school students for why their elementary teacher had such a strong impact on their lives.

>　　*…She knew each student individually. Like she'll sit and talk to everybody individually… she was like a teacher and a friend. We could talk to her about anything we wanted to….*

>　　*…some kids was like struggling in homes and stuff in our class… she was like our mother when we came to school… And that's what's so special about her.*

Teachers' Beliefs About Why Children Misbehave

Some barriers to caring, trusting relationships stem from teachers' beliefs about children. While most teachers enter the profession because they like and enjoy children, many also have beliefs about human nature that make it difficult for them to form caring relationships with children who regularly misbehave. Deeply imbedded in our culture and in traditional approaches to discipline and classroom management is the belief that children behave badly because they don't see behaving well to be in their self interest. For example, the authors of one traditional discipline system argue that children could behave well *if they just wanted to*. Therefore, they assert that it is the teacher's job to get them to want to behave well by promising rewards for desirable behavior, and unpleasant consequences for undesirable behavior.

If a teacher views misbehaving children as not trying or not caring enough to behave well, it will be more difficult to trust in the good will of students and to feel nurturing and caring toward them. Such a view of children can lead one to become angry and respond punitively when students misbehave. It can also lead one to misperceive innocent behaviors as intentional misbehaviors. Believing that children willfully misbehave out of defiance or laziness can drive a wedge between teacher and students, even generally well-behaved students. Consider the following example of an interaction between John, a generally well-behaved student while in Laura's classroom, and his high school math teacher. I asked John if he had ever gotten in trouble in high school, and if so, to tell me about it.

> Yes I have (gotten in trouble at school.) It wasn't that bad. ... I said something to the teacher, she said something to me, I started talking back and she sent me out of the classroom. I had to go to ISEP (in school suspension), but just for one period. I came back for the rest of the day.
>
> I came in late, I was like 30 seconds…, maybe a minute late to the classroom. I can't say (exactly). ... And she's like: "Why you late?"
>
> I said, "My locker wouldn't open."

And she's like, "Go get a note from security."
And I'm like, "I had to go to the office to get my locker opened."
She said, "You got to get a note."
I said, "Why, just 'cause my locker wouldn't open?"
She said "Get out of my classroom or I'll write you up."
Now, I'm mad because why am I getting written up when my locker wouldn't open. I'm only 30 seconds late and…I got mad, really mad.

This teacher's requirement that John leave the class to get a note confirming the truth of his explanation carried a clear message of mistrust. John reacted with anger to the mistrust and to what he perceived as an unreasonable demand on the teacher's part. John's display of anger in questioning the reasonableness of the teacher's directive led the teacher to send him to in-school suspension.

In the process of describing this incident, John offered his own analysis of why the interaction happened and why it ended badly.

I didn't really know that teacher that well and she didn't know me that well. We didn't know each other. The chemistry wasn't good.

…(If this had happened in Mrs. Ecken's class) I probably would have said "Yes mam." I wouldn't have had an attitude. Just because of the relationship.

> **"students have been found to be more likely to follow rules that they don't personally find reasonable if they have a good relationship with their teacher"**

John's analysis points to mutual mistrust—student mistrust and teacher mistrust. He says that he would have complied with the teacher's demand even though he believed it unreasonable, if he had had a trusting relationship with the teacher. This idea is supported by research. For example, students have been found to be more likely to follow rules that they don't personally find reasonable if they have a good relationship with their teacher

(Nucci, 2001). However, teacher mistrust is probably an even more important cause of this unpleasant interaction.

If the teacher had a more trusting view of students, she would have accepted John's explanation for his tardiness, the whole unpleasant interaction would have been avoided, and John would not have missed the day's instruction. Teachers' mistrust of students can lead to the use of more control, more often. The over-use of control denies students their needed autonomy, leading them to resent the teacher and to be less willing to

> *"The over-use of control denies students their needed autonomy, leadning them to resent the teacher and to be less willing to follow the teacher's directives"*

follow the teacher's directives, especially any that the students perceive as unreasonable. Teacher mistrust can make it more difficult to build trusting relationships with generally compliant and trusting students, like John, but it can lead to disastrous consequences with students who enter the classroom with a mistrusting attitude themselves. For these students mutual mistrust can lead to confrontation after confrontation and an escalating relationship of defiance, control, and disrespect.

This brings us to the third major impediment to nurturing, caring, trusting teacher-student relationships: students' beliefs about themselves and others and their relative lack of social and emotional skills.

Students' Emotional Skills and Beliefs About Themselves and Others

Some barriers to caring relationships stem from the mistrusting attitudes students bring to the classroom. In every classroom there are at least some students who have learned from past experience to mistrust themselves and others. It is no easy task to form a caring, trusting relationship with students who themselves have not learned basic trust.

For a variety of reasons, often having to do with the nature of children's early relationships with their primary caregivers, some students develop a belief that others cannot be trusted to provide for them and even that they themselves are not worthy of care (Sroufe, 1996; Pianta, 1999). Such early caregiver-child relationships are called "insecure." For example, some caregivers are over-controlling or punitive, some are inconsistent, unresponsive, or simply unable to meet their child's needs. Children in such relationships are unable to trust that their caregivers will provide for them. Consequently, they create alternative strategies for getting their needs met and coping with interpersonal relationships. Depending on a number of factors, these strategies might involve withdrawal, helplessness, passive aggression, constant attention seeking, overt aggression, defiance, bossy assertiveness, and manipulation.

Often, these students will have underdeveloped emotional skills. They will be quick to become frustrated or angry and will have little ability to delay gratification or monitor their own behavior. Their lack of self control will result in many annoying and disruptive behaviors— shouting out, rushing to be first in line, taking forever to settle down to work. Additionally, their lack of trust will lead some to be clingy, manipulative, and attention seeking and others to be defiant, aggressive, and controlling in their interactions with peers as well as teachers. Some test our patience, seemingly going as far as they can to avoid doing what is expected of them. It is difficult to like such students, and having to deal with their annoying behaviors can leave little patience for relationship building.

Overcoming Barriers to Warm, Caring, Trusting Relationships

Structural Barriers

There is not much that the individual teacher can do about the structural barriers to forming trusting relationships (overly high academic expectations, high-stakes testing, large class sizes). However, it is sometimes possible to ameliorate the effects of these barriers by increasing the amount of time teachers have with children. Keeping students in a self-contained classroom for all or most of the day increases the time teachers have to get to know their students and build relationships. Choosing to have lunch with small groups of students periodically can provide non-stressful opportunities to talk with them, build personal knowledge, and create mutually friendly feelings. Setting aside time simply to talk or play with individual students when there is no academic agenda can help build mutual liking and good will. This might be before school, during recess, while other students are working individually, during class free time, or after school. Finally, keeping students for more than one year, either by moving up a grade or two with students or teaching a mixed-age class where the younger students enter and stay for two or three years, can provide the extra time needed to build understanding and caring, trusting relationships.

Teachers' Beliefs

Fortunately, the structural barriers to trusting relationships are less important than barriers that are within the control of teachers—their beliefs about children. I am not saying that beliefs are easy to change, but at least our beliefs are within our control. The common belief that children are primarily self-interested derives from Behaviorism, an outdated psychological theory. Current research in human motivation and the role of childhood attachment in children's development paints a very different, more complex picture of children's needs, motivations, and development. Research across ages and cultures substantiates that, in addition to food and safety, humans have at least three basic psychological needs—autonomy, belonging, and competence (Deci & Ryan, 1985). Furthermore, as a species we are more highly motivated toward cooperation than competition (De Wall, 2005). However, to develop our capacity for cooperation and the emotional skills needed for successful learning and cooperation, infants and children need a secure relationship with a loving and guiding caregiver. Most children experience a secure relationship with their caregivers and, in that relationship, learn to trust themselves and others, regulate their emotions, and engage cooperatively

> *"... in the view of current theory and research, children want to learn"*

with others (Sroufe, 1996; Stayton, Hogan, and Ainsworth, 1971).

Overall this research provides a different, more positive view of children and their motivations. Children are not by nature lazy, motivated only by the promise of pleasure or the fear of pain. Instead, in the view of current theory and research, children want to learn (provided they see the learning as relevant to their lives and they believe they can succeed). They also want warm and caring relationships with their caregivers and their peers. Just as with academic competencies, children need help with social, emotional and moral skills and understandings in order to learn and behave well. Like all humans, children also need reasonable autonomy; most can be trusted to strive to do their best, when given the freedom and guidance, to make their own developmentally appropriate choices. If one views children in this way, one is less likely to focus on controlling children and more likely to focus on helping or guiding them.

Of course children need adult control as well as wise guidance. We need to create safe environments in which children can interact with reasonable freedom and we need to be there to prevent problems when their self control or other social, emotional and moral competencies are insufficient. But even then, we will be more successful if our focus is on support, guidance, and instruction, rather than control. In a nutshell, children want to learn, to please, and to cooperate if they are in an environment where their needs for autonomy, belonging, and competence are being met. Indeed, research across many cultures demonstrates that children actively seek adult help to learn the skills, customs, and guiding principles of their culture (Tharpe & Gallimore, 1988; Rogoff, 1990). Children are predisposed to trust that caring adults can and will provide the guidance they need to acquire the knowledge, skills, and understandings for successful life in their community. For adult guidance to be optimally successful, adults, in turn, need to trust that children will willingly use their guidance with minimal external control or enticement.

The research supporting children's cooperative nature is strong. However, children do not always appear cooperative in the classroom and it is not easy to believe in their cooperative nature when faced with classroom discipline situations. Consider the following incident that recently happened while I was serving as a volunteer aide in my grandson's second grade class.

The children were in a line coming back to the classroom from the library. The teacher was at the front and I was at the back. Just as the teacher and children were entering the classroom, Mark, a student who often pushes the limits of authority, pushed Chloe, causing her to fall to the muddy ground. Chloe was unhurt, but her clothes were covered in mud. I pulled both students aside, while the rest of the students went into the classroom with the teacher.

I asked Mark and Chloe to tell me what happened. Apparently someone bumped into Mark, he mistakenly thought it was Chloe and so shoved her back. Unfortunately for both of them, the shove was hard enough to cause Chloe to fall to the ground.

I tried the standard tactic of asking Mark what else he could have done if he thought that Chloe pushed him. No answer.

I then asked him why it wasn't a good idea to push Chloe. To this he replied, "You'll get in trouble." I asked him for other reasons, but he would say nothing more.

I stressed that he was not in trouble, that I was just trying to help them solve the problem created by Chloe being pushed down and help them avoid similar problems in the future. I asked him if there was some way he could make it up to Chloe for pushing her to the ground and getting her clothes muddy. He just stared at me with no answer. (I thought, I'm getting nowhere with this boy. At that moment, I did not believe in his desire to be cooperative. Instead, I thought, "He's stonewalling me.")

So, I turned to Chloe and asked her if there was something Mark could do to make her feel better. She said, "He could say he's sorry."

Mark, however, would say nothing. I found myself starting to feel angry at Mark as I struggled to come up with a way to turn this situation in a positive direction. It was then that I said to myself, "Remember, he wants to be cooperative." As soon as I thought this, I began to see Mark differently. He now looked more frightened than defiant. Frightened of me, of what he had done, and frightened that he really was going to get in trouble.

To gain more time to think of a way to bring about a positive result, I suggested we go into the classroom. Once there, I asked Mark to sit at his desk, which, to my surprise, he willingly did. I got him a piece of paper and wrote two questions, How can I help Chloe know that I'm sorry? And "What else could I have done?" I asked him to choose one to answer in writing.

Mark pointed to the first question and then asked if he could draw a picture first. I hesitated, but I didn't want him to feel trapped or punished so I said yes. He drew for a while but soon it was time for recess and snack. He asked if he could go get his snack and I said, "Yes."

When Mark returned, he quickly wrote that he could tell Chloe he was sorry and continued with his drawing. It was now time for the students to go to different classrooms for reading. Mark and Chloe are in the same reading group. Mark said, "I don't want to go to reading. I just don't feel like it."(At this point, I believed that Mark was struggling to be cooperative and probably afraid to face Chloe.) I put my arm around him and encouraged him to go to reading, saying that he'll feel better once he has had a chance to tell Chloe that he is sorry. Mark agreed and went off to reading.

When the class returned, Chloe was wearing clean clothes brought by her mother. When Mark entered, the first thing he said to me was, "I haven't had a chance to tell Chloe yet." (Chloe was in the office waiting for her mother to come with clean clothes when Mark had gone to look for her and she hadn't returned before he had to go to his reading class.)

He then went up to her, said he was sorry, she graciously accepted his apology, and both settled into the classroom routine.

Even though I knew better, I had come very close to acting on the erroneous assumption that Mark wasn't sorry for pushing Chloe down, and that he was being defiant and "stonewalling" me. We naturally feel frustrated when students seem to defy us, harm others, or show disrespect. Frustration can lead to anger and undue power assertion. This time, my theory based-belief, that children want to be cooperative but often lack the needed skills and understandings, helped me control my anger. I was then able to focus on *helping* Mark find a way to make amends with Chloe, rather than on *making* him do so.

> *"Adopting a view of children as cooperative rather than self-interested... helps us look for ways to work collaboratively"*

Adopting a view of children as cooperative rather than self-interested, and as intrinsically motivated to learn rather than requiring extrinsic rewards or punishments, helps us look for ways to work collaboratively with students. When we see students in a more positive light we will allow them more autonomy and feel warmer toward them, which, in turn, will help them trust us. But finding a way to provide students with some choice and autonomy while preserving a moral community where everyone is safe is not always as easy as it was in the situation with Mark and Chloe. Some children are so deeply mistrustful and angry, or so accustomed to fending for themselves through manipulation and power assertion, that they will not respond positively to suggestions and guidance. This brings us to the third barrier to warm, caring, trusting teacher-student relationships: students' beliefs about others, themselves, and the nature of relationships.

Students' Beliefs

As described above, not all children believe that it is wise or safe to be friendly and cooperative and not all want or believe that they can learn what we have to teach. For the most part, these are the children who have not yet learned to trust. They are using every skill they have to survive in a world where they believe others cannot be relied upon to meet their needs. And to make matters worse, the behavior of these children makes it hard to like them. It is difficult to like students who are clingy or constantly seeking attention. It is even more difficult to like those who are defiant, aggressive, manipulative, and constantly pushing or testing limits. It is tempting to avoid unnecessary interactions with children who are constantly seeking attention and to use power assertion to force defiant or oppositional children to follow our rules. However, such responses generally serve to confirm these students' mistaken views that we cannot be trusted and provide them with evidence that they need to persist in the very behaviors we are trying to stop.

> *"...if we use the lightest control possible while assuring the children that they are better than their unacceptable behavior indicates, we will begin undermining their own negative views"*

These children present teachers with quite a dilemma. Focusing our efforts on the children's beliefs rather than their behaviors provides a way out of what otherwise might become an escalating series of battles. Trying to change attention-seeking behaviors by withholding our attention is likely to lead to increased attention seeking or hopeless withdrawal. More troubling, controlling aggressive or defiant behaviors through power assertion, especially power assertion accompanied by unpleasant consequences, is likely to result in behavioral control, but at the cost of trusting relationships and willing compliance. Still, the behaviors of these children will frequently need to be controlled. However, if we use the lightest control possible while assuring the children that they

are better than their unacceptable behavior indicates, we will begin
undermining their own negative views of themselves. We will also begin
building their view of us as trustworthy. Unlike most of the children in
a classroom, these children will be very slow to trust.

I am not arguing that power assertion is unnecessary. Power
assertion is not inconsistent with a caring stance (Noddings, 1992).
Laura frequently had to rely on power assertion, especially with her
defiant and angry students. But to overcome the mistrustful views of
these students, power assertion needed to preserve as much autonomy
as possible and convey as much respect and consideration for the
student as possible.

To help clarify this point let us look at an actual example of
Laura's use of power assertion when these students were in elementary
school. This example involves Tralin, a student with a history of
fighting and teasing classmates; it occurred during Tralin's second year
in Laura's classroom. Laura had been working hard to build a trusting
and supportive relationship with Tralin and many of Tralin's positive
characteristics had begun to emerge. However, Tralin still had a quick
temper and sometimes used forceful ways to get what she wanted.

In this incident, the children are getting ready to leave the
cafeteria. Tralin shoves another student, Tyrone, out of line so she
would be able to stand near her friend, Ella. When Tyrone complains,
Laura simply tells Tralin to give Tyrone back his place in line and
proceeds to move the class out of the cafeteria. Basically, Laura trusted
Tralin to correct her own behavior based on a verbal reminder that her
behavior was unacceptable. Here, in Laura's words is what happened
next.

> Before we could get all the way outside, she (Tralin) was
> screaming at Tyrone, "Your mom uses crack cocaine! Your mom's a
> crackhead!"

> I asked her to just step aside so we could talk. I asked her why she
> had called his mother that, and she said, "Because she is and he lied on
> me and said I pushed him out of the line and I didn't touch him."

I said, "You know, Tralin, you're lying to yourself. I saw you push him out of the line. You wanted to be with Ella and so you shoved him out of the way.

"You know I'm not going to allow that, and I'm not going to allow you to call his mother names. Can you imagine how painful it is for Tyrone to know that about his mother, to suffer all the pain from that, and then to have to be at school and have you make his pain even worse? That's just not right."

The simple directive did not work and led to an even more harmful act on Tralin's part. At this point Laura sees that she needs to be more forceful. She begins by directing Tralin to step aside and asking for an explanation of her behavior. Laura refuses to accept Tralin's denial of wrong doing, accusing her of lying to herself. Laura clearly states that she has the power to keep Tralin from harming others and she focuses Tralin on the harm she has caused to Tyrone, hoping to arouse Tralin's empathy. Next Laura briefly considers a punitive consequence, shaming Tralin by calling her grandmother. However, she quickly reconsiders and instead offers Tralin the opportunity to make reparation to Tryone.

I asked her if she thought that maybe we ought to call Granny and let her know that this is what she's doing in school, but what really needed to happen, I thought, was for Tralin to make it up to Tyrone in some way. I said, "You know, you said some ugly things to Tyrone and I think it'd probably be best to take care of that."

She just looked at me, so I said, "When you have a plan, just find me and let me know, but I think that you should take care of it before the day's over."

Again, Laura demonstrates trust that Tralin will do the right thing and she affords Tralin the autonomy to come up with her own plan and, to some extent, in her own time. This time, Tralin rises to Laura's trust.

About an hour later Tralin came up to me and kind of stood there, so I asked her if she had a plan. She said, "I need to tell him that I'm sorry and that I didn't mean any of it. I was just mad and that's why I said it."

I asked her if she wanted him to come out in the hall so she could tell him that privately, and she said, "Yeah, but first I need a drink."

I told her, "Listen, you go get a drink and I'll tell Tyrone you want to talk to him in the hall."

When Tyrone came back in, he was happy and so was Tralin (Watson & Ecken, 2003, pp 162-163).

In sum, this disciplinary encounter ended up being more about instruction than power assertion. Laura helps Tralin see Tyrone's perspective and think about how hard his life must be. She calls upon fairness, and then tells Tralin that she should try in some way to repair the harm she has caused. Power assertion was clearly involved and there are real consequences for Tralin, but they are not designed to inflict discomfort on Tralin. They are designed to induce empathy and moral feelings and provide Tralin with a way to right a moral wrong. Laura not only shows respect and confidence in Tralin by letting her figure out a way to make reparation, she also displays empathy by asking Tralin if she would like to talk with Tyrone privately. In the end, this disciplinary interaction, an interaction in which Laura exerted control over Tralin, ended with Laura and Tralin feeling more trust in one another. Their relationship strengthened rather than weakened.

Second Principle
Support/Encourage Friendly Relationships among Students

Almost all of the high school students spontaneously commented on the friendly nature of their elementary classroom, frequently contrasting it with their experiences in middle and high school. For example,

That class was, no hands down, the best class of my years, I mean since I been in school. … we did things together. Everybody knew everybody and everybody was a friend to everybody.

Everybody was like in one big group because everybody knew each other.

…as our class grew and everything we became like… one big happy family, I guess you'd call us.

> *"… how Laura handled discipline encounters was probably the most important factor in building friendly relationships among her students"*

Teachers have many ways to foster friendly student relationships, for example, engaging students in cooperative activities, providing opportunities for students to talk together and exchange personal information, encouraging students to help one another, and conducting regular class meetings. Laura did all these things when these students were in her elementary classroom. They are described in *Learning to Trust.*

However, how Laura handled discipline encounters was probably the most important factor in building friendly relationships among her students. Although Laura sometimes became angry, generally she handled discipline calmly with respect, explanation, and guidance. Sometimes students perceived that they were being punished when, for example, Laura would direct a student to leave their table or the group in an effort to preserve a productive learning environment. But far more frequently discipline encounters did not engender angry or hurt feelings in the students. And it is these respectful, non angry discipline situations that the students remembered seven years later. Laura's respectful approach to discipline contributed to an overall atmosphere of respect and friendly feelings among students. For example, Paul, a quiet and very well behaved student who did not ever misbehave, remembers Laura's disciplining of others as follows:

> *She doesn't really get mad she'll just try to talk it over with 'em. …*
> *I thought she would really get mad, but after seeing her face I could see*
> *that she wasn't really frustrated with the person.*

Cindy, also a quiet and very well behaved student who, like Paul, simply did not misbehave in the classroom also described Laura's approach to student misbehavior as friendly and respectful.

> *She has like a little bench by the window. She'd usually take them*
> *over there and sit down and talk with 'em. …She … wasn't harsh. She*
> *just explained to them what they did wrong, that it's not acceptable and*
> *all that.*

When all students, even students who frequently misbehave, are treated with respect, friendly feelings are engendered throughout the class. This general feeling of respect is captured in the students' comments above declaring that "everybody was a friend to everybody" and that the class was "one big happy family." It is also captured in the following comment by Paul:

> *There weren't really no(sic) bad kids in that class.*

When no one is seen as "bad," everyone is a potential friend.

In addition to setting a general tone of respectfulness, discipline encounters can also ameliorate hurt feelings and actively support the building of friendships between quarreling or angry students. Consider the situation above in which Tralin pushed Tyrone out of line and when asked to give Tyrone back his rightful place proceeded to call his mother a "crack head." Not only was Laura and Tralin's relationship strengthened by the disciplinary interaction, so also was Tralin and Tyrone's. Had Laura followed her initial instinct to embarrass Tralin by calling her grandmother rather than helping Tralin empathize with Tyrone and make reparation for her misdeed, it is likely that both students, Tralin and Tyrone, would have come out of the encounter with bad feelings toward the other: Tralin blaming Tyrone for the unpleasant consequences that befell her, and Tyrone angry at Tralin for pushing him out of line and taunting him about his mother.

Third Principle
Use Student Misbehaviors as Opportunities for Social, Moral Instruction

You did what you did, you got in trouble, next day come back, act like nothing happened. You know, just start all over again.

This description of classroom discipline offered by Tralin reflecting on her high school classroom experiences might sound like a positive report of school life. She might have been saying that her teachers don't continue to hold students' misbehavior against them. That once you accept your punishment you can come back to class with a clean slate and "just start all over again." However, that is not what Tralin is saying. She continues by contrasting discipline based on punishment followed by a clean slate with her elementary teacher's approach to discipline.

> *"... her elementary teacher's focus on ethical instruction was more helpful and effective than punishment"*

(In my elementary school classroom), if we got in trouble…(my teacher would) give us a chance to think about it… How could we change the situation?… What could we have done to make it better? You know, things like that.

What Tralin is saying is that her high school teachers fail to use occasions of student misbehavior as opportunities for moral or ethical instruction. Instead, they treat misbehavior as something to be controlled through moderate punishment. Sometimes these moderate punishments made Tralin and the other students angry, especially if they felt the punishments were unfair. But more importantly, Tralin is pointing out that her elementary teacher's focus on ethical instruction was more helpful and effective than punishment.

Tralin is speaking from personal experience, but there is a substantial body of research that supports her position. Research in family socialization supports the role of disciplinary responses in moral learning and development. Martin Hoffman (2000) offers two reasons why parental disciplinary actions are important for children's moral growth: 1) such encounters are frequent, at least for children between two and ten, and 2) they provide parents with highly salient opportunities to teach the misbehaving child how to respond morally in a moral encounter. Several studies have found significant correlations between parental discipline and children's moral development (Hoffman, 1960, 1963, 1975, 2000; Hoffman & Saltzstein, 1967; Zahn-Waxler, Radke-Yarrow, & King, 1979). For example, parental discipline strategies that are low in power assertion and involve instruction and empathy induction (a focus on the harm the child has caused to others) relate positively to children's concern for others and a general prosocial orientation. Alternatively, a heavy emphasis on power assertion and punishment are related to higher levels of aggression and antisocial behavior.

> "... a heavy emphasis on power assertion and punishment are related to higher levels of aggression and antisocial behavior"

In the classroom, where disciplinary interactions are also frequent, teachers play a similar socialization role. If teachers view discipline as primarily about instruction, empathy induction, support for ethical behavior, and reparation, their responses to student misbehavior can foster ethical development as well as create order and prevent harm.

When misbehaviors pose the possibility of, or cause, harm they offer particularly powerful opportunities for moral learning. Student-student conflict along with behaviors like teasing, name calling, excluding, laughing at someone's efforts, stealing, and threatening harm, provide teachers with the opportunity to develop many skills involved in ethical behavior, e.g., perspective-taking, self-control, and communication skills as well as empathy, moral sensitivity, and moral understanding. And because the other students are often watching, those who have not caused harm are absorbing some of that learning along with the misbehaving student or students. However, such learning is unlikely to happen if the misbehaving student is simply informed that his or her behavior was wrong, and then punished, even if the punishment is commensurate with and related to the misbehavior.

> *"... such learning is unlikely to happen if the misbehaving student is simply informed that his or her behavior was wrong, and then punished, even if the punishment is commensurate with and related to the misbehavior"*

Punishment, however, is difficult to abandon. Not only is the socialization role of punishment ingrained in our culture, our legal system is also built around punishment. Sometimes it is argued that since children will be punished when they are adults if they break the law, they need to learn in elementary school that punishment follows misbehavior or rule violations. However, children are not adults. They are still learning the competencies and understandings required for mature ethical behavior. As I argued above, more often their misdeeds are the result of lack of skills and understanding, not lack of will. We are sometimes inclined toward punishment because we grew up with the idea that if children are not punished for their misdeeds they will keep on doing them as long as they are in their self-interest. This view of punishment guides many formal approaches to classroom discipline. When the field of classroom management was being developed, Behaviorism was the dominant psychological theory guiding educational practice. One of Behaviorism's core assumptions is that organisms are motivated solely by self interest. Given this belief, it makes sense to cause an unpleasant consequence to follow a child's misbehavior as a means of convincing the child that the misbehavior is really not in his or her real self-interest. But the view that children are motivated solely or even primarily by self-interest is not consistent with modern research on children's motivation and development. While children, like all of us, are motivated by self-interest, they are also

> *"... punishment as an inducement to ethical growth is at best ineffective and at worst counterproductive"*

motivated to form caring relationships, to help and cooperate with others, to explore and learn. These other motivational systems make punishment unnecessary. Not only is punishment not necessary for convincing children to abandon their misbehaviors, it can impede children's ethical growth.

The Problem with Punishment

Punishment is harm purposefully done to someone who has caused harm as a response to the harm. In the school setting its purpose is usually to induce in students the desire to act in accord with school rules and expectations by having them experience the negative consequences of failing to do so. From a developmental perspective, punishment as an inducement to ethical growth is at best ineffective and at worst counterproductive. A punished person may avoid the punished behavior in order to avoid future punishment, but avoiding personal harm is not an ethical reason and thus the better behavior is not the result of ethical growth. Also, as Martin Hoffman has argued, punishment can cause the punished to focus on the harm done to him or her, lead to resentment of the punisher, and take the focus off of the harm the child caused others. For most children, who generally want to be good but may be lacking the skills or understanding to be so, punishment is unnecessary. Their social, emotional, and ethical skills or understanding are lacking, not their desire to be good. Punishment may stop the behavior, but when the misbehavior is the result of insufficient skills or understandings, the use of punishment squanders an opportunity to teach the needed skills.

For oppositional children, those who have little trust and a confrontational stance toward the world, punishment may temporarily control the particular behavior, but it is likely to reinforce their untrusting, defiant stance and justify in their mind future aggressive, defiant behavior (Hall & Hall, 2003). Further, the teacher's relationship with such students is likely to be undermined, limiting the teacher's effectiveness at supporting the student's academic as well as ethical development.

Alternatives to Punishment

So what is a teacher to do when one student or a group of students misbehaves? There are clearly times when teachers need to use power assertion to control student misbehavior. From a developmental perspective, the teacher's goals when dealing with misbehavior are to preserve his or her relationship with the student and provide whatever support the student needs to stop misbehaving. With a conception of students as generally wanting to learn and wanting to be in mutually caring relationships, teachers need to guess at the possible causes of the misbehavior, take action designed to address the potential causes, and judge the effectiveness of their actions. For example,

- Is the misbehavior caused by the student's lack of social or emotional competencies? Explain or teach the missing competency and support the student in the exercise of the underdeveloped competency.

- Is it caused by an untrusting and aggressive stance toward the world? Build a caring relationship and teach the child that he or she can trust you and others.

- Is it caused by frustration at not being able to succeed at the assigned academic work? Alter the assignment or provide extra support or encouragement.

- Is it caused by feeling rejected or unappreciated? Display affection and respect for the student and look for ways to encourage good feelings and friendship from other students. And so on.

Let us look at some typical classroom misbehaviors to see what these alternatives responses might look like and how they might play out. Common classroom misbehaviors fall into several categories:

• Academic misbehaviors:
Expending little effort to accomplish learning tasks, failing to turn in assignments on time, failure to do home or classroom assignments, not paying attention during instruction

• Trust violations
Stealing or taking other people's things, lying, going to the bathroom to avoid classroom work, cheating or copying

• Mistreatment of peers
Teasing, fighting, name calling, pushing, bullying, annoying, ignoring, bossing

• Classroom disruption
Talking or other distracting behavior, failure to raise hands during class discussions

• Disrespect/defiance of adults
Refusal to follow directions, stomping off in anger, refusing to answer questions

• Classroom or school rule violations
Running or talking loudly in the halls, not coming to school, misuse of playground equipment

There is not time or space to discuss the potential causes of all misbehaviors and possible alternatives to punishment for each. However, the general principles can be illustrated by discussing possible responses to a few typical misbehaviors from the first three categories. Detailed discussions regarding other misbehaviors can be found in *Learning to Trust*.

Academic Misbehavior:
Failure to Do Home or Classroom Assignments

Failure to do home or classroom assignments is a common misbehavior. Common punishments for such misbehaviors include lowering a grade, making the student spend recess or time after school doing the assignment, and not placing a sticker after the student's name on a prominently displayed wall chart. None of these common responses is likely to bring about willing compliance or solve whatever is preventing the student from doing the work. From the perspective of Developmental Discipline, the teacher's goal is to persuade and enable the student to do the assigned work. If this behavior happens very infrequently, a caring response would be to remind the student of the importance of doing assignments and give the student a little extra time to complete the work. However, if a student frequently fails to complete in-class assignments, or turn in homework assignments, the teacher's job is to try to find out why, in order to work with the student to solve the problem that is keeping him or her from fully engaging or completing assignments.

The first consideration needs to focus on the nature of the assignments. Are they too hard or too easy? Are they engaging and relevant to the students' interests? Will the work help build needed skills or knowledge? If the answer to any of these questions is, "No." then adjusting the assignments is the first step. If the answer to all these questions is yes, then the focus turns to how to help the student engage with and complete the assignments.

For homework, is the child's home environment chaotic or unsupportive? If the teacher guesses this to be the case, he or she might discuss with the student ways to find space and time to do the homework. As a last resort, the teacher might offer to let the student come into the classroom before or after school or during lunch to work on homework. If, on the other hand, the student is not completing the homework because it is too difficult or taking too long, the teacher might work with the student to adjust the homework to something the student can do in a reasonable amount of time. Teacher and student might even agree on a time limit for the student to work and at that time the homework is done, completed or not. The amount of homework assigned in elementary school has increased dramatically over the last 20 years, and some educators, Alfie Kohn (2006), for example, have argued that there is no evidence that it supports student learning. In his recent book, *The Homework Myth*, Kohn argues that homework can actually hinder academic development by undermining intrinsic motivation. Checking to be sure that homework assignments are likely to benefit the student and can be completed in a reasonable amount of time is an important first consideration.

If the homework is reasonable and likely to benefit the student, and the student is not completing it because he or she is watching television or playing computer games, the teacher might try working out a schedule with the student that builds in special homework time. If this is the problem, it will likely take weeks before the student manages to resist temptation and actually do the homework on a regular basis.

More difficult is the situation where the student is not doing homework because he or she thinks that the work is boring or too easy or unchallenging. The teacher might sit down with the student and listen to his or her complaints. If the student convinces the teacher that the homework really is not beneficial, the teacher might agree to find more suitable homework. If, after discussion, the teacher believes the homework really would help with the student's learning, the teacher can explain to the student how, in the teacher's mind, the homework will help the student. If the student remains unconvinced, the teacher can ask the student to trust him or her or strike a compromise with the student. For example, the student may be asked to do half of the homework and the teacher and student jointly choose another academic activity to supplement for the remaining half. There is no single solution. It does require trusting the student and at the same time vigilance and firmness so that the student's learning is fully supported.

What a lot of possibilities, and we have only addressed a student's failure to do homework! Punishment is a lot simpler. But punishment carries with it the assumption that students do not want to do their work or have no good reason for not doing the work. Developmental Discipline asks teachers to take a different attitude toward students—a believing attitude. If we believe that students want to succeed, want to be in a caring relationship, and want to learn, then we can try strategies that might overcome potential barriers and help students complete their homework or class assignments. Below is an example of this approach to undone homework from a talk given by Joy Pelton to the Teacher Education Department at California State University at Sacramento.

> *"Developmental Discipline asks teachers to take a different attitude toward students—a believing attitude."*

…the "belief system" or attitude you bring into a relationship with a child can make profound changes in that child's life.

I believe a story one of my student teachers shared with me on Friday might illustrate this. She has a student in her fourth grade class whose father is in jail for child molesting and whose mother is by all accounts barely functioning. At school the boy is friendless. He comes to school without being prepared with homework, books or classwork. He often does not participate in class and rarely does any work. When asked why he does not bring in his assignments from home and why he does not participate in class, he is silent and shrugs his shoulders. His regular teacher makes him stay in every recess to make up his assignments. The student teacher told me that she thought he liked to stay in at recess because he didn't have to deal with kids on the playground. In any event, staying in had had no affect on getting him to bring his materials from home, or doing his work in class.

My student teacher was prepared to teach a science lesson on Thursday and anticipated that this boy would not have brought to school the science packet the students were working on and should have taken home the night before. She agreed with the ideas discussed in our discipline and management class about children's needs of autonomy, belonging and competence. She believed that he wanted to be a part of the classroom community, that he had a need for belonging and also a need for competence.

> *"... she consciously changed her attitude toward him by trying to relate to him in a believing way"*

The day of her lesson, she made another copy of the science packet, and before she started the lesson, she gave it to him, saying, "I made a packet for you this morning before school so you could participate in the lesson today." He looked up at her with such gratitude and surprise that she was astonished at the effect of her gesture. She told me that for the first time this year he completed his work during the regular class time. She wanted to discuss this incident with me because she wasn't sure exactly what had taken place with the boy. The only thing she felt she knew for sure was that prior to Thursday, she had seen him as a child who should be punished for his behavior. But before her lesson, she *consciously changed her attitude toward him by trying to relate to him in a believing way*—with the belief that he did want to participate and to succeed. Her gift of a new packet, and of entering into a relationship with him in a believing way changed his and her reality. (Pelton, 2000, emphasis in the original)

Trust Violation: Stealing

Let us move now to consider stealing, a relatively common misbehavior that violates interpersonal trust. There are three somewhat interrelated reasons why children take things that do not belong to them. One is that they really want the object and do not have enough self control to keep from taking it. A second is that they do not really understand, at least at the time they are taking something that does not belong to them, how they are hurting someone else. And thirdly, they do not quite understand the importance of trustworthiness to maintaining trusting relationships. Of course it is the teacher's duty to stop students from harming or stealing the property of others. However, our job is also to build into students the understanding of how stealing hurts others and the community as a whole and to help them develop the self control that will enable them to keep themselves from stealing. For some students, one instance in which they have been caught stealing and simply helped to see how the stealing violated the bonds of trust will be sufficient to keep them from stealing again. For others, this lesson is difficult to absorb and will need to be repeated many times. Consider the case of the missing Pilgrim Doll in Laura Ecken's classroom.

On Thursday, this little girl Molly, who is mainstreamed into our class for about 90 minutes each afternoon, brought in a little Pilgrim doll. And it disappeared. We kept looking for it but it didn't seem to be anyplace in the room. I asked the kids a number of times, "Does anybody know where it is," "Has anybody seen it?" And no one had. So finally I asked my instructional assistant to just go out and see if it was in anybody's locker. And he found it in Tyrone's locker. Somehow Tyrone had managed to get that little doll out of the classroom and into his school bag in his locker.

A little later when the class was busy with other things, I asked Tyrone to come outside. Nobody knew why we went outside. I said, "Tyrone, I know that little doll is in your locker. Can you tell me about it?" And he said, "I like it and I want it." And I said, "It's not yours." And, you know, he looked me straight in the face, and was upset that I knew he had it, but he looked me straight in the face and he goes, "I want it. It's so nice." And so, I said, "Tyrone, you can't keep it. It's not yours."

Now, the day before he had brought this tool in, it's like a ratchet. It had these thing that stick on the end, I don't even know what they're called, but they tighten different size bolts. The other kids loved it. So I said, "You know, you brought that in yesterday and it's been here for two days. And what if somebody in our classroom decided they really liked it and they just took it home?" He just stared at me. He didn't say anything. And I said, "What would you think about that?" And he wouldn't answer. And I said, "It's not theirs, is it?" He said, "No, It's mine." And I said, "Well, that's like the Pilgrim doll. It's not yours. It belongs to Molly. She brought it in to share, and you can't take it." So finally he got it out of his locker and handed it to me.

And then, it was like a miracle, Molly walked out of the classroom to get a drink of water. Tyrone took the little doll from me and walked over to her and handed it to her. He told her, "I really wanted it. I really liked it. I'm sorry I took it." She said, "That's all right, you can hold it the rest of the day if you want."

At this point I didn't want to take any chances and it was almost dismissal time, so I just said, "That's really nice of you, Molly, but it's time for you to go back to your other classroom, so you better take your doll with you now." And she did.

Laura prevented Molly from losing her doll and in the process she began helping Tyrone understand the moral principle of reciprocity by helping him see that since he would not want others to take his things, it is not right for him to take things that belong to others. In the end, Tyrone gave Molly back her doll and apologized on his own initiative. However, this was just the beginning of a long process to help build Tyrone's moral understanding and self control. Additional occasions involving Tyrone taking things that did not belong to him are described in *Learning to Trust*. Each time Laura stressed the unfairness of taking others' things and tried to help Tyrone see the harm stealing does to his classmates and his community. Eventually the stealing stopped. No punishment was ever necessary.

Understanding that you should not steal because you would not want someone to take your things is an important step in moral development, but it is only the beginning of a true moral understanding of why stealing is wrong. Stealing, like lying, is a violation of the bonds of mutual trust. In the following example of classroom stealing, Laura helps John understand that stealing is a violation of a trusting relationship.

> We were going down to special area. Haley Monroe (another teacher) called and asked to borrow some seashells. I told her that I'd run them down to her. So I set the jar of seashells on my desk because we were going to special area and I asked Cindy to run them down to Miss Monroe when we get back from special area.

> On the way out of the room, John was at the end of the line, and he reached his hand in there and took one. Well, David saw him put it in his pocket. David followed him to his locker which was on the way to special area. John was standing there looking at the shell and David said, "John, what are you doing with that?"

> John said, "I found it on the floor and I was looking at it." And David said, "Well, that's Mrs. Ecken's. Don't you think you ought to give it back to her?" John just stood there. David said, "Well, do you want me to give it back to her for you?" And John said, "Yeah."

> This all happened toward the very end of the day. So, the next morning I talked to John and he said, "I found it on the floor." I said, "No, John, now let's just talk honestly. You took it out of the jar and you stuck it in your pocket." He teared up and his face turned real reddish. I sighed, "Why, why did you do that?" And he said, "I wanted one."

I said, "Well, you know what, I have tons of them. If you wanted one, you could've just asked me for one. And the funny thing about it is, if you'd just asked me for one of them, I would've given it to you. But getting in a situation like this with somebody you really care about… It doesn't make me feel very good that you would do that." And then he started crying. I said, "And it looks like it doesn't make you feel very good either." And he said, "It doesn't. So I said, "Well, you think of how you're going to make this up to me and I'll talk to you before you leave at the end of the day."

When it was time to leave he had not said anything to me about it. As the kids were going down the ramp and I was saying good-bye and reminding them to walk home carefully, John ran back up the ramp. He hugged me and said, "I'll never take anything else from you. That's how I'm going to make it up." I said, "Okay, I believe you. If you need something, talk to me about it." And then he just went on home.

One might think that stealing a shell from a whole jar of shells was no big deal. But John took something that belonged to someone who cared about and trusted him. Laura very gently helped him see that his act constituted a violation of their relationship and her trust in him. John's shame and guilt were consequences of being caught stealing, but they were not punishments. Nor was Laura's asking John to think of a way "to make this up" to her a punishment. Rather, it provided John with a way to restore trust and repair their relationship.

Mistreatment of Peers:
Name Calling or Physically Harming Peers

When misbehavior causes harm, for example, teasing or bullying a peer, it is important for the teacher to do more than stop the behavior and provide moral instruction. The teacher also needs to focus students on the harm they have caused, a true consequence of their behavior; encourage the students' empathic response to the other's distress; and insist that they find a way to repair as much as possible the harm they caused.

> *"... focus on the harm they have caused... encourage the students' empathic response to the other's distress... insist that they find a way to repair as much as possible the harm they caused"*

As the vignette described earlier involving Tralin calling Tyrone's mother a crackhead demonstrates, truly facing the negative consequences of one's actions can provide a powerful force for ethical growth. Providing or requiring the offending student to repair in some way the harm done is an important next step.

Depending on the student and the strength of the student-teacher relationship this process can look very different. Sometimes it may only involve a sincere apology. And, as the example above in which Mark pushed Chloe to the muddy ground demonstrates, it may be difficult to orchestrate even that. Just as with supporting a student's academic growth, supporting moral growth requires knowing what individual students are capable of, believing that they want and can do better, and helping them reach a little farther than they might on their own. Like developing number sense, learning to work effectively with others in kind, fair, and collaborative ways, is a slow, multifaceted process that is accomplished more quickly by some students than others. There is a lot to learn. Here are just a few examples:

- the ability to recognize, understand, and control one's own emotions
- the ability to read and understand the perspective and emotions of others
- peaceful ways to meet one's needs
- effective communication skills

Developmental Discipline's principle tools:

- **reminders**
- **guidance**
- **explanation**
- **instruction in social or emotional skills**
- **empathy induction**
- **requests for reparation**

For some students, it will also require abandoning an aggressive, confrontational view of the world and learning to believe in the good will of others as well as one's own self worth.

The classroom and school setting present many opportunities for many different kinds of misbehaviors. Developmental Discipline's principle tools for preventing, stopping, or ameliorating student misbehavior—reminders, guidance, explanation, instruction in social or emotional skills, empathy induction, and requests for reparation—will usually be sufficient to maintain a caring classroom environment conducive to serious academic and ethical learning. However, the right approach for individual children in specific situations will not always be obvious. Guiding the ethical development of frequently misbehaving students will require considerable patience, fortitude, trust in the student's intrinsic motivation, and trial and error. Sometimes it will seem like you and a particular student have made no progress at all. But a continued respectful stance toward the student, along with continued efforts to convey a caring attitude toward the student, are likely, in the long run, to have a positive effect. If you are lucky enough to have the student for more than a year, you may even see this positive growth for yourself.

However, you may not. But even if you do not, the supports for eventual positive growth may be moving into place.

Consider the case of Martin. As a seven-, eight-, and nine-year-old student Martin presented Laura with many challenges. Here Laura reflects on her struggles to help Martin.

> First of all, I know I'm in an area of service. I know that my job is to serve these children in any way that they need. And, I guess, here's where I'm having difficulty knowing what to do—Martin is having so much trouble.

> I have a goal to support him. So I can do that and get done what he needs, but it's usually at the expense of everybody else. I can take care of Martin and try to make situations that he can deal with and be successful in, but how much can I do that at the expense of the rest of the class?

> I know it's my job to teach that child, and I know it's my job to do anything and everything humanly possible to make him successful. But I'm at the point where all I do is think about him. He consumes me.

Laura tried many different strategies to help Martin learn to control his temper, stop teasing and bullying his classmates, and generally be more considerate and respectful of her and his peers. But it seemed to Laura to require constant effort. There were times when she felt she had no choice but to require Martin to leave the classroom. Sometimes Martin's behavior was so disruptive that Laura felt she needed to send him to a special class for students classified with behavior disorders. But Laura never gave up on Martin; she continued to work with him in collaborative, non-power assertive ways whenever possible. Although he made considerable progress in her classroom, Laura was never confident that Martin would be able to successfully manage himself in less supportive settings. When he moved on to fifth grade and then middle school, Laura worried that his behavior would spiral out of control.

But Martin's behavior did not spiral out of control. When I met with the principal of Martin's high school, he described Martin as a "fine young man." And Martin's self description—what he hoped another would say about him—was consistent with the principal's view of him.

> *I'm a good, funny person... I really never got into much trouble. I always did what I was told...I always have a smile on my face. Always. ... And I like sports.*

In his high school reflections Martin attributes much of his success to Laura.

> *I used to have a bad attitude until I got Mrs. Ecken. She changed that... She's the one who really got me into sports... Doing good in school. Staying out of trouble in school... I guess focus on my work more. Try to make it somewhere in life.*

And although Laura had to use power assertion on numerous occasions to control Martin's behavior, what Martin remembers are the far more frequent collaborative and supportive interactions and the many pleasant times he had in her care.

> *She was nice, real nice. She was my favorite teacher of any teacher I ever had... she used to do a lot of things. She used to take us places. She was real nice. Sometimes she would get upset at something. She would just sit down and explain to us. Like when me and Terry got into an argument, she would just say, "Now you all are best friends. You don't need to get into an argument." We used to get into arguments all the time... If she was here... I wish she was teaching here.*

When asked to give advice to new teachers, Martin stresses the importance of a collaborative trusting relationship and its long-lasting positive impact on him:

> *Try not to be too hard or too easy on the students because that*

makes them real frustrated. I guess, to be like Ms. Ecken, really... try to keep the students out of trouble. Help them to make goals like Ms. Ecken did. They have to make goals in life. That's what I did.

...I make goals all the time. Do this. Do good in school. Make good grades so I can graduate. So I can be the first one of my mother's kids to graduate.

While Martin's memory of his experience in Laura's classroom is idealized, what is important about it is that it is a memory of a mutually trusting relationship. Sometime in the course of their time together, Martin came to trust that Laura really cared about him and could help him become a good and successful person. Martin's remembrances and his eventual success stand as proof that even a defiant and angry student can learn to trust, and continue to grow ethically and intellectually, building on the foundation laid in elementary school.

Summary

Creating the ideal classroom conditions for the support of ethical growth is not easy, but succeeding at doing so can have long-lasting positive effects. The elementary school and classroom are ideal environments for learning the skills and understandings needed for living an ethical life in the complex social world outside the family. Taken together, observations of an ethically oriented elementary classroom, interviews of high school students who had been in that classroom, and current developmental and motivational research, provide three principles to guide teaching to support ethical growth. These principles for guiding classroom teaching are identical to principles derived from research in family socialization. Children develop prosocially and ethically when the adults in their world:

- Build warm, caring, trusting relationships with them.
- Support and encourage friendly relationships among their peers.
- Use their inevitable misbehaviors as opportunities for social and ethical guidance or instruction rather than punishment.

While elementary schools and classrooms offer powerful opportunities, teachers face several barriers in their efforts to implement these principles in support of the moral growth of students:

- Structural barriers such as large class sizes, limited time with students, and increasing pressures for higher levels of academic performance make it more difficult to take the time to get to know and build caring relationships with students.

- A common but unsupported view of children as motivated solely or primarily by self interest makes it difficult to view children in a positive light, especially when they misbehave.

• Children's underdeveloped social, emotional, and moral competencies and the untrusting, oppositional or demanding attitudes some children bring with them to the classroom can create serious management problems, try our patience, and make it difficult to build trusting relationships both with and among the children.

There is relatively little that teachers can do about the structural barriers to building caring, trusting relationships with students except to look for small ways to increase personal time with students individually and collectively. Likewise, there is relatively little that teachers can do about the level of social and ethical competencies and the untrusting or oppositional attitudes some students bring to the classroom. However, teachers can overcome the third barrier by consciously revising their view of children. Shifting from the common Behaviorist view of children as primarily self interested to a view of children as wanting a caring relationship, wanting to learn, and wanting friendly relationships with peers can significantly change the climate of the classroom. Consciously adopting such a "believing stance" can lead one to lessen the use of power assertion replacing it with working collaboratively with students to guide their behavior in positive directions.

> *"Realizing that children have basic needs for autonomy, belonging, and competence, teachers can organize their classrooms and set up their management practices to honor and support these needs"*

Realizing that children have basic needs for autonomy, belonging, and competence, teachers can organize their classrooms and set up their management practices to honor and support these needs. By so doing, they are themselves modeling an important ethical principle, showing concern and respect for the needs and rights of others.

Likewise, by trusting in children's good will, teachers can view social or moral misbehaviors in the same light they view academic mistakes—as occasions calling for guidance, support, or instruction.

There are many ways to integrate support for ethical growth into standard curricula and instructional strategies. For example, choosing and discussing works of literature with ethical themes, involving students in defining and upholding school, playground, and classroom guidelines, highlighting ethical issues in social studies and the heroic or ethical behaviors of historical figures, and engaging students in collaborative learning activities are all ways to build ethical understanding and skills. However, classroom management and discipline strategies provide the most frequent and powerful opportunities for ethical guidance and instruction.

Sometimes that guidance or instruction can simply focus on the building of specific skills or understandings—teaching fair decision-making strategies to disagreeing students. However, sometimes, particularly for deeply mistrustful children, that guidance needs to focus on students' faulty beliefs as well as their relatively undeveloped social and emotional skills. Changing students' basic views of the world, their ability to trust others and themselves, is a much longer process involving sometimes heroic efforts at relationship building, occasional use of power assertion, careful teaching of skills, trial and error, and patience. What it does not need to involve is punishment. There is no guarantee of success, but the success of many of Laura's students is testimony to its possibility.

References

Deci, E. L., Ryan, R. M. (1985). *Intrinsic motivation and self-determination in human behavior.* New York: Plenum Press.

De Waal, F. (2005). *Our inner ape: A leading primatologist explains why we are who we are.* New York: Riverhead (The Penguine Group).

Hall, P. S. & Hall, N. D. (2003). *Educating oppositional and defiant children.* Alexandria, VA: Association for supervision and Curriculum Development.

Hoffman, M. L. (1960). Power assertion by the parent and its impact on the child. *Child Development*, 34, 129-143.

Hoffman, M. L. (1963). Parent discipline and the child's consideration for others. *Child Development*, 34, 573-588.

Hoffman, M. L. (1975). Moral internalization, parental power, and the nature of parent-child interaction. *Developmental Psychology*, 11, 228-239.

Hoffman, M. L. (2000). *Empathy and moral development: implications for caring and justice.* New York: Cambridge University Press.

Hoffman, M. L. & Saltzstein, H. D. (1967). Parental discipline and the child's moral development. *Journal of Personality and Social Psychology*, 5, 45-57.

Kohn, A. (2006). *The homework myth: Why our kids get too much of a bad thing.* Cambridge, MA: Da Capo Press.

Nucci, L. (2001). *Education in the moral domain.* New York: Cambridge University Press.

Noddings, N. (1992). *The Challenge to care in schools: An Alternative approach to education.* New York: Teachers College Press.

Pelton, J. L. (2000). "Taking a believing stance." Lecture given to Department of Teacher Education at California State University at Sacramento.

Pianta, R. C. (1999). *Enhancing relationships between children and teachers.* Washingtron, DC: American Psychological Association.

Rogoff, B. (1990). *Apprenticeship in thinking: Cognitive development in social context.* New York: Oxford University Press.

Sroufe, L. A. (1996). *Emotional development: The organization of emotional life in the early years.* New York: Cambridge University Press.

Stayton, D. J., Hogan, R., & Ainsworth, M. D. S. (1971). Infant obedience and maternal behavior: The origins of socialization reconsidered. *Child Development, 42,* 1057-1069.

Tharp, R. G., & Gallimore, R. (1988). *Rousing minds to life: Teaching, learning, and schooling in social context.* New York: Cambridge University Press.

Watson, M. & Ecken, L. (2003). *Learning to trust: Transforming difficult elementary classrooms through Developmental Discipline.* San Francisco: Jossey-Bass.

Zahn-Waxler, C., Radke-Yarrow, M., & King, R. (1979). Childrearing and children's prosocial initiations toward victims of distress. *Child Development, 50,* 319-330.

About the Author

Marilyn Watson, Ph.D., recently retired from the Developmental Studies Center, where she headed the center's National Teacher Education Project and was the program director for the Child Development Project (CDP). The Child Development Project has been called one of the most successful moral development programs ever implemented. Watson has spent the past two decades working with educators to promote children's social, intellectual, and moral development. In a recent CSEE moral development training session with Marvin Berkowitz, Berkowitz called Marilyn Watson "the master of classrooms for moral growth." She is the author (with classroom teacher Laura Ecken) of *Learning to Trust* (Wiley, 2003).